Perfectly Imperfect

Perfectly Imperfect

NAVIGATING A TEENAGER'S UPS & DOWNS IN LIFE

Authored By,

Saisha Singh

Disclaimer

Registered Office- 907-Sneh Nagar, Sapna Sangeeta Road,
Agrasen Square, Indore - 452001 (M.P.), India

Website: http://www.wingspublication.com

Email: mybook@wingspublication.com

First Published by WINGS PUBLICATION 2023

Title : Perfectly Imperfect

Price : Rs. 499 | AED 40 | $ 10

ISBN : 978-93-6006-540-9

LIMITS OF LIABILITY/DISCLAIMER OF WARRANTY

Dedicated to

Mama, papa and didi

Acknowledgements

Writing a book is harder than I thought it was, but more rewarding than I could've imagined. None of this would have been possible without my parents, who pushed me out of my comfort zone to try new things. They made me believe that nothing was impossible, and supported me though every step. The amount of growth I witnessed in myself in the book writing process was eye opening. Like always my parents supported and guided me through this journey, even when I was being uncertain. Mama was the one who always encouraged me to write short stories and be creative since my childhood. I thank my sister for being the first person to read my book as well as Harshita aunty, for giving her valuable feedback and support in this valuable journey. And finally, Ankita aunty for being my inspiration, without whose support this book would not be possible. I want to thank God most of all, because without God I wouldn't be able to do any of this.

I thank all my friends for sharing their experiences with me, which become an integral part of this book. I am grateful to Dr. Kailash Pinjani for his support along with his expertise, thank you Ms. Chinmayee, the editor for giving me feedback on every chapter, lastly, I would like to thank the Wings Publication team for all of their help in making my dream possible. I want to conclude with a special mention to, my parents, Dr. Neeru Sood and Dr. KK Singh and, my cousin sister Sunidhi Kashyap for always staying by my side though my ups and downs.

Preface

When I first decided to write a book, I knew right away that my book would be a sincere attempt at making teens my age know that they are not alone. This book is meant to help my readers navigate through some of their situations and problems. It is inspired from issues that me and my friends faced while entering adolescence and staying true to our values and authentic selves. Reading this book will be like talking to a friend who relates to you and offers advice. I hope it gives you comfort in some situations you might be facing and lastly you know that you are not alone.

Index

Chapter : 1

Fast Forward

" Teenagers are more alike than they are different."

Do you ever think about how our parents were when they were teenagers? Sometimes, that thought pops into our heads when we think about our experiences. We think about how did they act when they were our age and what experiences they went through. There is obviously going to be a difference between their teen phase and ours.

Not just them, it is the whole 'Gen X' population. They were born between 1965 to 1985. So, their approximate ages are from 43-58 years old. Generation X is known as the middle child in its comparison between baby boomers and millennials. They were the first generation to grow up with cable television available.

While reading about people from other generations discussing their teenage life, I noticed it wasn't fundamentally different from some issues faced by teenagers today. Of course, there are some major differences, like how the previous generations grew up with less influence of technology in their daily lives.

So, because of no phones, they would have way more free time than we do today because today's generation is just on their phone 24/7.

They wouldn't sit on their laptops or computers. They did not have as much strict supervision as we have today, they spent most of their free time outside with their peers and thus also being more physically active.

My mother is also a part of Generation X. Teenage days were mainly her and her family. She was close with her family, her parents and her sisters. Her family was important to her. But unlike today's world, where kids are very open to their parents and share everything with them, she was not very open with her parents. She had developed a fear of sharing things with her parents. She did not want to share anything private with them. But they were still very close.

But on the other hand, she had her siblings, her 3 sisters. They would share everything together and have a close bond. I can also relate to this, I have my cousin sister, who is basically my sister. I share absolutely everything with her, I trust her.

Because the children were not open with their parents, their parents were not able to guide them in life. Because of this, the kids made a lot of bad decisions, thus going down the wrong path. But the difference between their generation and today's generation is that now kids are more open with their parents, parents know what kids may be going through. Whenever the child is struggling, they at least tell their parents about what is bothering them so they can get their parents' help.

She used to go to a co-education school, meaning there were both boys and girls in the same school. Because of this, the interaction between guys and girls was normal, and it was not awkward between them. They would openly interact with them.

While discussing with my mother, I found out she was raised in a joint family. So, she had a lot of support while growing up, like her grandparents, who gave her lots of love and support. But the disadvantage of this was that there was no privacy among the family. If anyone made a mistake, instead of just being afraid of their parents, they would be scared of the family.

Unlike back then, kids mainly grow up in a nuclear family now, meaning it is just the kids, their parents and siblings. Living in such a household, you have more privacy and more space for yourself. Having more privacy means being more comfortable. Nowadays, kids are closer to their parents at home, interacting more and spending more time with them.

How teens used to spend free time before and now is quite different, now, it is usually sitting at home, watching any show or movie, staying on your phone for a while, or being on social media. Back then, they didn't have access to all these things, so going outside with friends, listening to music, or just spending time with their family was the typical activity to do when bored.

Impacts of social media, back then, there was barely any exposure to technology, there was no Instagram, Facebook, Twitter. Back then, everyone was more focused on studying, there wasn't much of a distraction. There was no negative influence on teens back then because of devices or technology.

There is an obvious difference between technology back then and today. Today's technology is more advanced, yes. It is better and more helpful, yes. But is it causing harm to the teens of today? Yes. There are so many disadvantages of social media in today's world. It has a lot of advantages in the medical field, and in AI.

The impact of social media on teens is not just based on body image or beauty standards, there's more to it. Firstly, the amount of time wasted. So many people waste time just sitting on their butts all day long and being lazy, their eyes glued to the phone every minute of the day. Back then, they would go out most of the time, have fun and spend a lot of time with friends. But nowadays we don't go out that much, they are usually confined inside the house.

Because of devices, kids start to procrastinate. How does this happen? Because when kids start to study or start doing some work, the temptation of trying to use their devices is always there. There are many instances of mine as well. Before, as soon as I would start to do an assignment for even 10 minutes, I would think, "Oh, that's good enough for now, I'll do the rest later." and then I would start watching a show or movie on my laptop for hours, until I realised, I had like 3 hours left for the deadline, and of course, we all work best under pressure, right? But that's not a good practice to do, though.

As we grow, more and more work will pile up for us, and if we don't manage our time wisely and just waste it sitting around on our devices and being lazy, we aren't gonna with achieve our goals.

My dad was also born into a joint family. He had quite a similar experience to my mother. He was born in a rural area, meaning a small village. Even he had stated that there was no term as 'privacy' back then. He expressed that he was very open with everyone, there was no hiding of anything because everything was bound to come out at one point.

During his summer holidays, he would go out and have fun with all his cousins, playing 'kabaddi', 'gulli danda' and football outside. Plucking mangoes in season and all his relatives come over and stay for weeks during their holidays. He had a whole circle of friends with whom he would play with after school.

In his childhood, he did not spend much time with his parents, he said that from his 6th to 8th grade, maybe even till 10th, he didn't stay with his parents, he lived with his aunt and uncle, and they provided everything for his school. He would help them out in the field work and other household work.

Kids back then did not have as much freedom as they have now, parents were very strict, they could not make a lot of decisions by themselves, and they would have to follow everything the parents would say. Kids now have individuality. They didn't have many options to choose from for a future career, even parents were not aware of all these fields because they would stay in small towns, and they didn't have that much exposure to the outside.

Females were not as educated as today, only a few well educated families or wealthy families took their daughters education seriously. There wasn't much freedom for an individual to grow, you could do some degree and get a job, but now teens have so many facilities, even in school, we have so many training courses like coding, technology has made many changes in the thought process of parents as well as children, children have freedom to make their own choices. Simple living was the lifestyle. Back then, sisters would be each other's role models, they would follow them. Now people have better understandings, like before if being a doctor runs through the family, that means the child would have to become one too. Now, parents support children to pursue their passion.

How are our parents misunderstood often? We often tend to keep personal stuff to ourselves and not really reveal anything much to our parents, and because of that, our parents feel as though we don't feel comfortable enough to share things about our lives with them. So, they try to bond, but we sometimes neglect them when we are too caught up in our work, and that hurts a bit for them.

When your mom comes and tries to talk to you and asks you about how your daily life is going, you shouldn't get annoyed, she's just trying to take a break and spend time with you. They just want you to be open with them.

We don't notice these small acts that they do just to bond with us, we often misunderstand them when they are trying to tell us and guide us to the right path. There may be a difference in how our mindsets are from theirs, they may be a bit old fashioned, we should spend every minute we can with them, they can also feel alone at times.

Chapter : 2

Finding the right people

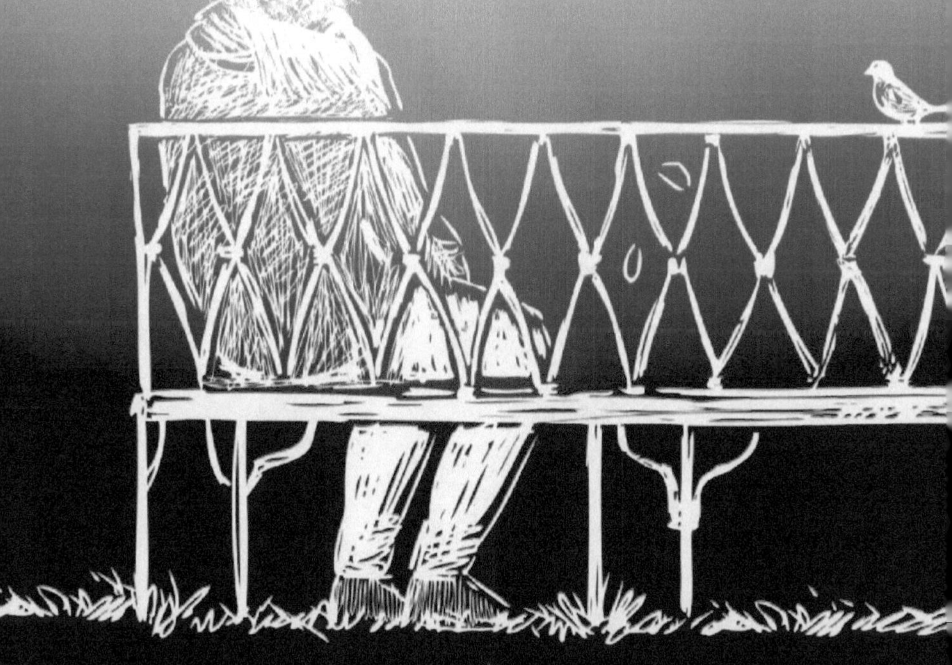

"Surround yourself with those who bring out the best in you, not the stress or the worst in you. One of the Keys to Happiness is to surround yourself with the right people. Changing your crowd can change your life."

- Jeanette Coron

When people say, "what is stress?" What is the first thing that comes to your mind? Is it maybe schoolwork or pressure to do things a certain way from your family? These are mainly the common types of stress for teenagers. There are a lot of levels of stress that people go through and the important thing is to know who to go to when dealing with stress. It is not easy to find the right people to support you or stay by your side through your tough times. When I say the right people, I mean people who know how to guide you to the right path. Everything takes time. But the one question that comes to mind is, "How do I find the right people?"

How do I know who to trust?

As I grew older I started to understand the importance of trust. You need to think carefully whenever you are going to trust someone. You need to make sure that they are loyal to you. You need to make a good bond with people you trust. You also need to show them that you are worthy enough for their trust as well. Like I said earlier it is not easy to find people who are pure and willing to support you in times of need. Its not easy to just make friends and immediately trust them, and if you do just know its not a coincidence, it was meant to be. They are the one for you. Everyone needs a shoulder to cry on and someone who motivates them for the best and not take them down the wrong path.

Trust is an important thing in life, without it people feel alone and helpless. This decision needs to be taken wisely and based on your past mistakes and lessons. Throughout your life you have probably had many people that you have talked about your problems to, but there is this one person to whom you tell everything. That person is whom you have the most trust in. You are comfortable with that certain person, you are ready to share anything with that person. That person is one of the most important people in your life. He/she guides you through your tough times. To pick people of good character, we have to first become a person of healthy character. This specific person can be someone from your family, a very close friend or even your parents.

Relying on friends and family

The type of difficulty you may be going through is sometimes stress. I say stress because it's common for our age group, usually stressing because of assignment due dates, or exams and tests. It's normal to be worried, but it's also important that you shouldn't be too stressed or worried about something. Your health could be affected if so. It's important to take care of yourself as well. Now in these times of need we need someone to lend us a hand.

I don't mean a tutor or a friend who simply tells you, "Its okay you can do it !", no, I am talking about someone who can actually help you. For example, whenever I used to struggle with coping with the stress of tests, instead of focusing and trying to study, I would text all my friends saying "Oh my goood, I feel so nervous for tomorrow's test, ughh what am I gonna dooo." And then I would simply wait for their response, usually expecting it to be, "Oh my god sameee, but don't worry we got this!!", because then I would feel like I am not alone feeling this way. In my case, instead of studying, yet again I would start procrastinating.

In my situation I didn't step out of my comfort zone and actually try to study or at least the bare minimum, to ask my parents to help me learn. But it doesn't always have to be your parents.

I found support from my cousin, she is the one always there for me. Whenever I was about to start procrastinating she would notice and say, "Aren't you supposed to be studying?", so I would then immediately go to study instead of sitting around and wasting my time.

These kinds of situations, in which you fall into trouble, is what makes you realise how important some people are in your life. These people can change your life, they can either make or break you. At your school as well, you should make good friends. Socialize with people, you should be nice to people so that they don't have a reason to be mean with you. Try to bond with people, go out and have fun with them. It is important that you should respect their opinions and they should respect yours. Cooperation is the key to success, right? People can change from time to time, either good to bad, or bad to good, the thing is, you should stay just good towards people. Don't let people grab an opportunity to look down on you. You should also always try to do your best in anything you do.

Whenever you are stressed, make sure to try to motivate yourself as much as you can. Try to get as much rest as you can. Eat and sleep properly. It is important to take care of yourself too. Like they say in a flight before taking off, “Before helping others put on the oxygen mask, put on yours safely first.”. You should also know what to share with certain people, and what not to. You will read more about this in the chapter, “Sharing may or may not be caring.”

Finding the right people, making a strong relationship, depends on you. Going to someone you feel comfortable with, expressing your thoughts and emotions, letting out all your feeling, that person should be the one, that person will listen to you and help you throughout your journey.

These people can help you in making decisions as well. If you are ever stuck in a situation you should also have someone tell you what is the better option. For an instance, once I was stuck in a situation where I had to make a decision, first I asked my close classmate what I should do, she casually responded to one of them. But then I though just in case I should ask someone else too, and well I asked my cousin and she told me to pick the second option. Turned out the second was the obvious best decision. Sometimes we should also have the ability to be able to make a wise decision. Thinking wisely, and focusing.

Avoid negative influences in life

In school, many incidents take place where a student, joins the wrong gang in the class, the troublemakers. An innocent student, who has no idea what she just stepped into. This would lead her to problems. That one gang which everyone knows, is the one full of students with attitude, arrogant, didn't care about studies, just going out and relaxing before exams. This certain group, the teachers never liked, this group is what could lead to a student going down the wrong path.

By influencing the student into doing wrong things, they could easily get more people into their "gang." You should be careful and aware about students like these, who don't care about school and act all full of themselves. These are NOT the right people. The right people will be loyal, kind, honest and caring. They may have flaws, because nobody is perfect, but they will still have these qualities. Stay on the good side of people, always be nice. It is never too late to change your qualities.

In conclusion

In simple words to summarize this chapter, have someone to help you in times of need, have someone you can talk to when you're stressed, have someone to lean on, have someone to stay by your side. Have the right person with you. Guide, mentor, family whatever you call them, they will help, you'll see. They will try to relate to your problems or situations and find solutions for you, or take examples of others. It is not necessary you have to tell everything, every single detail of your life to this person.

You tell them whatever you feel like telling them, you should feel comfortable. You shouldn't feel as though that person is forcing you to tell them everything. Knowing who and when to ask for help. This person, think of them as someone you can vent to, someone you can talk to about somebody else when you are mad, someone who won't judge you for you. That person may seem unideal, but no, it is very much ideal. These kinds of people, restore humanity.

Chapter : 3

Are they worth my trust?

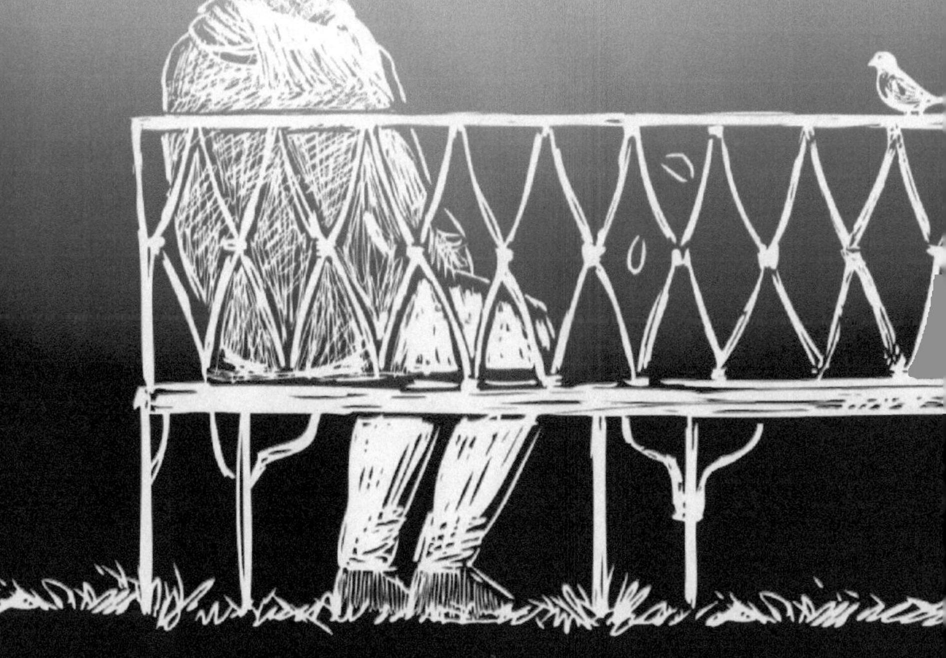

"While you are working to be trustworthy, your habits will change, and you will be reliable and have good character."

Trust is a key aspect of life, it is very important. Deciding whether someone or something is worth your trust is a critical judgment that can impact your relationships, decisions, and overall well-being. Trust is the foundation of any healthy relationship.

When someone is very honest and expresses their thoughts openly, that is one sign that they can be trusted. Meaning they will tell you everything and not hide stuff from you, as trust is easier to establish when there is transparency.

How to make out who to trust:

It also depends on the background, if you know about their past, maybe knowing that they haven't been involved in dishonest actions or behaviour. Checking by how they are now as well, you can make out.

When people make mistakes, they either admit to it or try to hide it. If they have made a mistake, do they take responsibility for their actions? And do they amend them when necessary?

Effective communication is also vital for trust. Seeing if someone communicates well with you, answers you, engages in conversations, and addresses situations and problems. Depends on whether they give vague replies or avoid communication.

Someone trustworthy, meaning someone who is worth your trust, their intentions matter as well. Do they have good intentions in mind? Values matter, too. Are they caring, kind, loyal and honest?

Trusting your gut is something you should do more. Listening to yourself or having a feeling that something isn't right about this person. Most of the time, your gut feeling turns out right. Your intuition can be a valuable guide.

You should know more about someone and any risks or consequences that could take place if you trust them. Could your trust be misplaced? <u>These are also some key factors to note.</u>

Asking people for advice, asking people is also a crucial point. Because then you could see that person from their perspective. Seeing them from another person's eyes, they can share opinions and their views, experiences and advice.

Since trust takes time, make sure not to blindly think you can't trust someone based on one or two experiences. People's actions change from time to time, and so will your trust based on those actions. Periodically evaluating that person's actions may tell you if you can trust them or not.

Trust is not an all-or-nothing concept, it is something that takes time, it is based on experiences, it is based on actions, it is based on observations. You also can't always guarantee trust, as I mentioned before, it may have a risk, so be careful while choosing people to trust, for your trust can be broken.

In the previous chapter, we went into detail about how to find the right people in life. After that, knowing if you can trust them is also very important. Having people to talk to is important in expressing thoughts and emotions. Venting helps mentally.

If you are someone who openly shares their feelings, it is good, but it is better not to overshare. People sometimes take this information and use it against you.

People coming to talk to you about their feelings shows that you are trustworthy, you are worth their trust. They are trusting you with their secrets. They believe that you won't reveal this information and keep it safe.

There are ways to develop trust. Being consistent helps, it shows the other you are there for them whenever needed. Respect, showing them some respect, treating them with kindness and taking their opinions and views into consideration.

Showing you are reliable to that person, thus building more trust. Paying attention and listening to them. This also helps in building more trust, this shows to the other person that you are interested in what they are saying and are paying attention to them.

If someone doesn't trust themselves, then it's nearly impossible for you to trust them. People who have more self-control shows that they are more likely to be trusted by others. Talking about self-control and temptations, if someone can't resist the temptation in any given situation or handle their impulses, it is going to be difficult to place your trust in them.

They are comfortable with making compromises for you, if you want something to change, they are fine doing it. This builds trust and forms the start of a good relationship.

Honesty and transparent behaviour show you can trust the person.

Trustworthy people do not make assumptions about others. They prefer not to get involved in gossip or rumours because that affects the person in question negatively. They would not try to bring someone down, instead, they would help them rise up. Showing their appreciation towards your actions and their gratitude as well.

How to be a trustworthy person:

Good and positive intentions. Showing you have good character and good intentions shows people that you are reliable and helpful. Shows that you are determined, and even if you fail, you try harder. With good character, you perform good actions, your actions speak louder than words, after all.

When you are shown as reliable, that means you have to keep your word. After all, they trust you, so you should keep your promises. Don't just give up if you are not able to do it under certain circumstances, talk to them instead and tell them why and try to make up.

Being kind, considerate, honest and compassionate are good qualities to have. Being honest is one of the best, although being honest is hard, it is for the best. It also helps you gain respect.

Being considerate is letting people know you are giving them another chance for a mistake that they made, being compassionate, respecting others' opinions and seeing things from their perspective.

Apologising to people when you have made a mistake is also very important. It shows you know what you have done, and you will work on it to make sure it doesn't happen again and make up for it.

Since people trust you with valuable information, it is important to keep it confidential and safe. They trust that you won’t reveal it.

Don't be dishonest or do actions that are not right, that may be a sign for someone else not to trust you. Don't gossip about others or get involved in spreading a rumour, this is wrong, if you start talking bad about someone, at one point, they will know and know not to trust you. This will make you look very much not trustworthy. Before talking bad about someone, stop and think for a minute about how you would feel if someone did that to you. It would not feel good. So trust me, and don't talk behind people's backs or make fun of someone.

Believe in yourself, too, at times when you feel down, know you are doing your best. Trust yourself and love yourself. Grow well first, then help others grow.

Sometimes, although you are being a good person, people don't appreciate your honesty and qualities. You should stay strong, and you should not start talking bad about them or spreading rumours.

Chapter : 4

The Listening Process

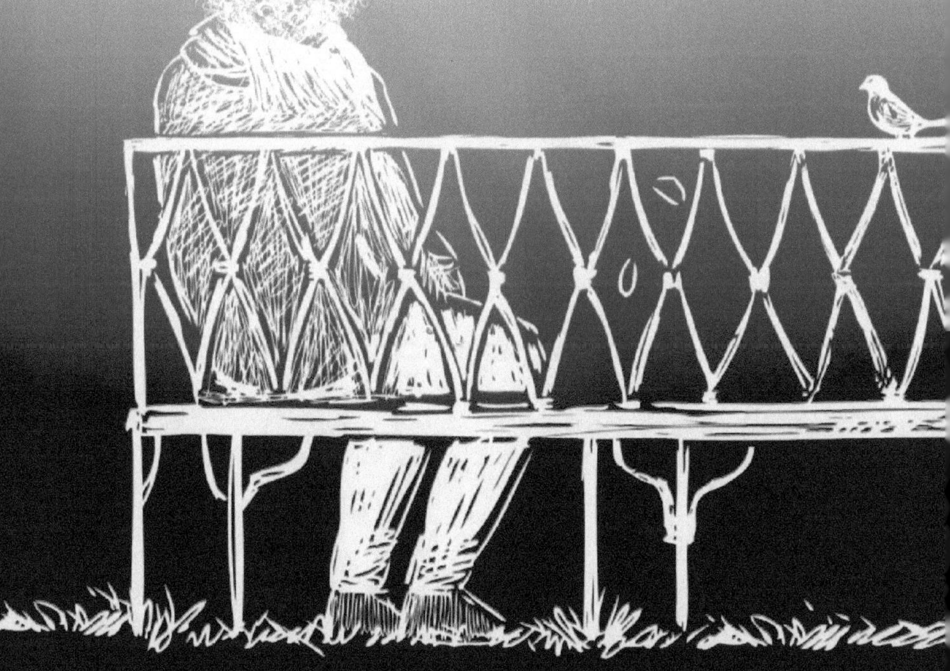

"Friends are those rare people who ask how we are, and then wait to hear the answer."

– Ed Cunningham

Listening and hearing are two different things. Hearing is just things going into your ear subconsciously. Hearing takes no effort, you physically experience sounds. Something you hear is like someone shouting from another room or a police car's alarm. When you listen, you put effort into it, you pay attention to that sound or someone talking. Hearing is passive while listening is active.

People can hear each other, but if you want to understand, you need to listen.

When in times of need, we go to someone for help, right? We talk to them, we explain our situation or what we are going through. They listen, process and try to find solutions to it. They are 'listening' to you. But if you went up to someone while they were distracted or busy and started telling them, they would not pay attention, that is 'hearing'.

Just listening to someone and implying what they said are two different things.

Whenever others are trying to tell you about what is troubling them, we should also listen and pay attention. It shows you are actually trying to help, you are trying to understand them.

Do people give you advice when you ask them? Whenever we ask someone for advice, we should at least try to use the advice they give us, right? When someone tells you any sort of solution, you listen to them, right? But is it necessary to always listen to them?

When you ask someone for help, you should know that that certain person will not judge you for what you say to them. They will try to understand instead of being judgemental about what you are going through. The same goes for you, whenever someone comes to you, you should let them know that they can tell you anything and that you will not judge them. Now that you know who are the right people and who are trustworthy, you should know if they are ready to help in ways whatsoever.

Listening and using people's advice can bring a lot of advantages as it is very valuable. To show that you are willing to get advice from them, you should first show that you are actively listening, like paying attention. When someone is giving you advice, make sure to stay open-minded to their suggestions.

When you are in a state of confusion, make sure to ask them, this also shows that you are actually interested and paying attention in the conversation. Show respect for the person giving the advice as well.

Not understanding something? Make sure to ask them clarify questions, this shows your genuine interest in their input. Another thing to make sure of is when you ask multiple people for advice, it can differ because it is from the views of different people. So, it is better to weigh out the perspectives and then make a final decision.

Trusting your gut is also a key factor, when you have certain inputs from different people, you should consider what is best based on your own judgement. After getting advice, you should think carefully and reflect on it. If you find advice that is good, but you don't think it will fit the situation too well, you should know how to alter it, you should be able to adapt it.

When someone gives you advice, you should show your gratitude towards them, especially if it turns out to work.

If the advice does not really help you, you should at least appreciate their intention.

After getting advice, you should know the final decision depends on you, you should get caught up in other words, after all, it is your call. As you grow, make sure to still be open to others advice. And keep an attitude of continuous improvement.

Listening to people's advice can be beneficial, it is a learning opportunity because usually, the advice given by people is based on their experience or if they have gone through a similar situation. When in a problem, asking for advice can help you, you can be creative with your thoughts, and it helps in problem-solving.

When you get validation from someone based on an event, it can help boost your confidence, they are words of encouragement. Asking people for advice can save time, instead of wasting time looking for solutions everywhere, when we ask someone, we can get ideas based on their knowledge and thoughts

Again, advice can help in better decision-making, it can help you make the right choices. Sometimes, accepting or admitting you wrong can be hard, so when you accept advice from someone, you should know that it helps in your personal growth and development of self-esteem.

When we go to people for advice, we try to look at a certain situation from a different view or perspective. So, when we ask others, we can broaden our perspective and improve decision-making skills by learning from others. With the help of this, the new things we learn help us later on and help build relationships as well.

To share my own example, when it is 11:30 pm, and I have just gotten into the bed, my cousin is also getting ready to sleep. She turns off the light switch, and my heart starts pounding. No, it is not because I am scared of the dark, I feel scared for some reason. I feel uneasy, and I lie on one side of the bed, staring out the window, the moonlight gleaming through the sheer curtain. I slowly turn around to see if my cousin is sleeping. She's just lying down with her eyes open; I slowly start to tell her what is bothering me, it's usually night time when all my problems pop up into my head.

Sometimes, it is about studying, like, "Oh no, I have an assignment due in like 30 minutes!" or it's about not preparing for a test. But it's not always this, sometimes it's for silly reasons, like I watched a scene of a horror movie by accident or I was sad because I was missing my parents who were in India.

But that is not what is to be focused on, what is important is that at least I had someone to go to and someone who listened to me without judgement. My sister is always open to whatever I want to tell her. She is my best friend, someone I share everything with. I trust her, and I'm pretty sure she trusts me too. She gives me a lot of advice, suggestions and tips to help me. She is always there to help me. These kinds of bonds don't happen overnight.

Good things take time.

When you are getting advice, make sure to look back and reflect on what kind of situation you are in. Considering the sources is also a key aspect, based on who gives you advice, you should evaluate the credibility of that person. If you get multiple responses, make sure to compare and contrast between them just to see the similarities and differences.

Don't take people close to you for granted, they are special and there for you to help you. They can guide you with wise inputs, when you ask people for advice, do not just casually take it and not think about it. Do not ask people for the sake of it. They are words of knowledge, they can help you in situations. Further in your life, you can use their advice as well.

When making a mistake with the advice given, you should know what went wrong and how not to do the same thing in any other situation. So, you can make better decisions in the future.

When trying to help others by giving advice, here are some things you can keep in mind it could be done:

- Firstly, only offer advice when someone asks, or you are close enough to just suggest it.
- Before directly giving advice, properly understand the situation and the state they are in.
- You should not be judgemental while listening to their problem, it should be a non-judgmental suggestion or approach.
- When you are suggesting ideas, give options or several approaches so that they can pick what is best for them in the given situation.
- You should also respect their decision, after all, they will decide what action to take.
- You should not overload them with too much information, it may confuse them, so just give simple and crisp points.

- If someone comes to you for advice, if you are hesitant and do not really know what advice to give them, be honest and tell them.
- Don’t force your ideas upon them, don’t be pushy, let them decide whatever they want to.
- If someone shares confidential information with you, make sure to keep it safe, as that person trusts you with that information.
- After giving advice, check in with the person to see how they are doing.
- Always stay supportive.

When giving advice to others, it is a way of providing guidance and support, know it is for their betterment, it is for their well-being, and you should empathise and respect them.

Chapter : 5

Sharing may or may not be caring

The outcome of oversharing is distrust, disconnection - and usually a little judgment.

- Brene Brown

When sharing things with someone, you should be aware of not going too far, sometimes, we overshare, so we should be a bit cautious. When you are really excited about telling someone about something or someone, you don't realise if we go over. People have boundaries, and sometimes, we should remember that we have them too, so we should probably stay in them. There are many people out there who can take advantage of excess information. They can misuse this information, and we would get into some sort of trouble.

Since we were kids, we've been hearing the phrase sharing is caring, which means if you care for someone, you should share things with them. We tell children to share because that can help them make friends, play and take turns negotiating with each other, and as we grow up, we still do this.

Sharing can take place in different contexts; for example, when you're in a relationship, because we love that person and we want them to be happy and grow. The act of caring and sharing also tells others that they should do the same so that the person receiving it also continues this.

Sharing helps us understand what someone is going through or when someone is in need, so this shows them that we care about them. Sharing is also a way to make you happy because when we share that experience with others, we also build a bond.

Sharing and caring are two different things. Sharing can be a way to care about someone or be considerate, but it depends on the context of what you are sharing. Genuinely caring about someone is showing that they matter, supporting them emotionally and understanding them. In the end, sharing is just a form of caring.

What should we not share? That's not a question that often pops up in our minds, but it's definitely something that we should know. When we think about what not to share, private information, certain passwords, medical details and stuff like these come into our mind. Well, it isn't wrong.

But there are other things as well, this is common among youngsters, people accidentally spilling secrets. When you are talking about something, you should also be aware of your surroundings, meaning the people around you.

Who do I share certain information with? Well, people you trust, right? But the thing is, it doesn't always go like this. Sometimes, people overhear or eavesdrop on conversations. They overhear information that they weren't. Like sometimes, it hurts people's feelings. Like talking bad about someone behind their back, and they get to know them.

Usually in school, people tend to have normal discussions with each other like with friends, so like discussing what they did over the weekend or if they went outside, what did they do, but other than that between like two or three friends or like a certain friend group they talk about things other than that because they're like close friends and they tell each other everything.

Who do I not share information with? When you're sometimes in public, and you're mentioning very private things to another friend of yours, it's most likely that someone is eavesdropping on your conversation and can hear everything that you're saying.

Don't share your information with people you don't

feel comfortable with. If someone forces you to share information, you definitely should not. Instead, go tell an elderly person about it, even in some families, they tell you not to tell people about like certain information. What information should you share with some friends? Not close friends but generally with your friends.

It is normal to talk about your daily life and stuff in general, but talking about something you are not supposed to mention out loud can lead to problems. For instance, it's a break in your school, and you're hanging out with all your friends, some friend of yours starts talking about some girl she doesn't like in the class, and everyone starts looking at her and behind her.

Guess what, the girl she was talking about, was right behind her. I mean, you shouldn't even be talking bad about anyone in the first place; things slip out of our mouths sometimes, and we can't control it. This is something everyone should work on. Stop, think about what you're going to say, and then speak, you should think carefully before you speak.

The most important thing, Once again, is to keep your information safe with you. It's also really easy for people to accuse you of things you didn't do. Sometimes, people close to you can use your own words against you, you should be really careful revealing information to people. Sharing too much information isn't good. If sharing private information, make sure it's safe and secure.

Who should I share my information with? Well, it's better to share information with people you trust, most of all like your friends and family. They can provide advice and act as a pillar of support for you... Usually, if it's a matter of your medical health or mental health, it's better to share things with your professionals, for example, your doctor or a therapist. When you're sharing information on social media, you should be really careful because it's information going out to the public. When in school or academic institutions, it's better to share work with your professors or teachers. And with online bots, if you're going to ask for information, you should be really, really careful not to share sensitive private information because who knows where that information could lead to. You should always take care of your private information.

When sharing, we should remember that everyone has boundaries, and we should respect them. As some people may not find it comfortable to share certain information, we should not keep persisting them to tell us. But sharing isn't always with information, it can also be sharing a certain responsibility. When that happens, make sure it should be fairly split so that someone doesn't feel as though it is a burden.

Don't share information with strangers, it could be anywhere. Online or in real life, it can lead to very bad situations.

Why should I share information with others? Sharing information with others can help in a few ways as well. Firstly, building relationships, when in a relationship, we tend to share information to build the relationship and strengthen it. It brings about trust and good communication, which is important in a healthy relationship.

In school, sharing information can help us grow. We can learn new things from others, and looking at their experiences, we can get creative and come up with ideas, it is a mutual relation; they tell us new things, and we tell them. At work or at school, we should share thoughts with each other based on any certain project or work we are doing. This can help in making more innovative ideas.

Sharing your feelings or empathy when a friend is going through a tough situation is also very helpful.

Chapter : 6

Am I too much?

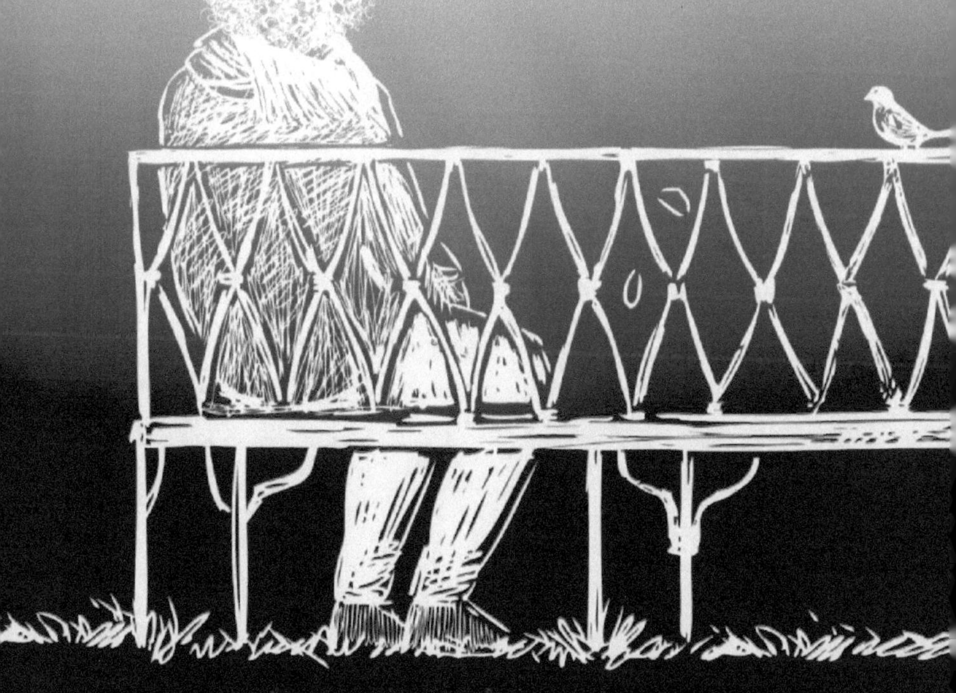

"We have to dare to be ourselves, however frightening or strange that self may prove to be."

-May Sarton

This thought often comes into our mind when hanging out with friends. When you are sometimes loud or too excited about something, they look at each other and give you looks. So, you have thoughts like, "Am I being too loud?". You shouldn't think about what others think of you.

No matter what they say or what they do, you should stay the way you are. If they comment about you or talk behind your back, you should ignore them, you do you.

Being self-conscious at this age is very normal.

You are always thinking about what others think of you. Today's society is just messed up. They judge you based on everything, your body, your clothes, your hair, your face. It's just the beauty standards of today's world. Listening to all this, so many people change themselves just for people and not for themselves.

Feeling like you are too much in front of people, you feel embarrassed, and you think, "They must think of me as weird, or too loud." But you shouldn't. Don't think about what they might think of you, if they judge you while you are just being yourself, cut them out. If you are close friends and they do it as a joke or playfully, you should know not to take it seriously.

Taking things seriously is another big topic. Based on either misunderstanding or just feeling hurt because of others. If someone tells you something mean or insults you, you sometimes take it to heart. It is normal to feel that. Sometimes, people are sensitive, and they are deeply hurt by someone's words.

'Judging' this word can be used in many perspectives. For example, in any survival shows or talent shows, there are judges to judge the contestants. When I say judging the contestants, they pay attention to the skills or talents that they have showcased. But in the case of between friends, if you judge someone, that means you judge their physical appearance or the way they act or how they are in general.

When you are conscious of yourself, you become anxious

about yourself and what others think of you. I used to often have these thoughts with friends. When I got my hair cut short, I was super nervous about going back to school. It was the first day, and I actually got a lot of nice comments. All my friends did make a bit of fun of me, but overall, everyone was nice about it.

If someone is telling you that you are overreacting, although you were just excited to talk about something, don't just sit there silent, sometimes you should stand your ground. If someone insults you, you should know to clap back and stand up for yourself. You need to gain courage, too.

Don't listen to people no matter what they say, listen to yourself, listen to your heart.

The same goes for you, you shouldn't judge people either, let people be how they are, and they will let you.

Sometimes, if you feel as though you are too much in front of friends, try to communicate openly. Share your feelings and opinions with them, hoping they will appreciate your enthusiasm.

Developing self-awareness is important, too, you get to know how you act and how you are and improve upon yourself. So is the self-examination, looking back at your behaviour, noticing why you feel a certain way, and if you dominate over conversations or cut off people while they are talking.

Channelling your negative energy from asking yourself, why did I do this or why did I do that, replace it with positive affirmations instead.

Sharing your feelings with someone close can also help you. Self-acceptance is necessary for you should be happy with yourself and how unique you are.

You should make friends, good friends to whom you matter, who trust you, and you trust them. They should stay with you no matter what happens to you. People usually stay with someone, but then when they are no longer interested in you or bored, they leave you. You should build strong relationships with people.

If you ever feel down because of someone's comments, make sure to spend some time healing. Do things that make you happy, that bring you joy from the inside. Overcoming your fear of trying new things is a big step. Because it involves making yourself realise you are good enough as long as you're happy. You should know you don't need to listen to what others say. You are you, and they are them.

If you are over excited and see your friends giving you looks, acknowledge it, maybe they feel overwhelmed by your excitement. If you feel you are being over by yourself, try mindfulness if you want to balance out your emotions.

Try talking to some people about it and addressing the issue, maybe they can have tips for you.

People have boundaries, and it's important to respect them, talk to them and, ask them if they feel you are crossing a limit when you are too excited and try to ask for ways for them to help you.

If you notice you or someone else is talking too much, and the others are silent, involve them in the convo and tell them to talk and share thoughts as well.

Seeing people's reaction based on your behaviour don't take it to heart, they don't wanna mention it, so instead, you understand it non-verbally. If you find it hard to control your excitement with people, seeking support can help you as well as people's feedback.

It is good to be energetic and happy, but it's also important to notice how that energy is affecting others.

What to do when you are overwhelmed, try to make a list of breathing exercises to do, this will help calm you down and relax you, as well as make you aware of your emotions and what you are currently feeling. Ask for help from someone you trust. Love yourself for who you are.

When people tell you to stop being so overdramatic, don't always try to tone it down, or try to change how you are acting. Instead, it's better to tell them, " I would appreciate it if you didn't judge me, I'm expressing the way I currently feel, whether you care or not". They wouldn't try to fight back because if you are strong enough and stand your own ground, nobody can tell you how to be you, and they would be slightly embarrassed.

Being too much is being too expressive, showing more emotions than others. It isn't a bad thing, it's being enthusiastic about something or just genuinely excited. Nobody should criticise each other just because of how someone acts or if they are too excited if you think about it.

Chapter : 7

Am I too less?

"Believe you can and you're halfway there."

-Theodore Roosevelt

At this age, it is normal to have a lot of burdens and expectations for many things. Doing well in school is one of our parents highest expectations. Because of all this, it causes stress. It makes you anxious and sometimes pisses you off. You think of why your parents are always scolding you for the smallest of things, you get annoyed easily.

Feeling like you are too less usually happens in front of mentors or parents. Feeling like you are a disappointment, feeling like you are not enough for them. Parents scold you for not doing well in school, going out to play for a very long time and not coming back when they told you to, sleeping for too long on weekends, and not studying hard enough. Disapproval from your parents and hearing their disappointment in you hits hard.

Because of that, the pressure falls upon us like thinking, 'I have to get full in this test.' Parents can be hard on you in many fields. Sometimes, it makes you feel like you are not enough. Situations happen in which you think they can only see your flaws, they don't appreciate you enough, only point out mistakes, and do not see what is right. But you should also know that amidst all their scolding, they are trying to lead you to the right path. Trying to help you understand what is right and what is wrong. Trying harder to make a better impression on your parents.

When they tell you something you did is not good, you feel the anger rush inside. Determined to prove them wrong, you try your hardest, yet they don't seem very much impressed. This is the case for some people, who, after many instances as such, just give up trying.

It is important not to be too hard on yourself, it can harm you mentally and physically tire you out. Know your worth, not everything has to be the best, you can try your best, and you do the most you can. That itself is enough that it is the best.

If you take their words seriously. They don't mean what they say. If they are angry or in a state of stress, they can blurt out things by accident that they don't mean. So, don't take their words to heart. Feeling like you are not enough.

Firstly, you should focus on yourself, you should not set ridiculously unrealistic standards for yourself.

Then, accept yourself for who you are. Instead of constantly telling yourself you can't do something, tell yourself that you are doing your best and that is enough. Going to friends and other family members can help you, they can support you through tough times. It is important to be able to control your emotions and your words when you are angry in front of your parents.

You should be careful not to say anything wrong towards them after all, they are your parents, and you should respect them. Mindfulness, breathe in and out, calm yourself down. When you feel like you will explode any minute because of how mad you are, start counting backwards in your head and distract yourself in your head.

Sometimes, if you are too stressed, go and do things that make you happy, like going out to the park, dancing, singing, listening to music, painting or doing art. You get mad because your parents get mad over small things, they take things too seriously? It is true that it happens, sometimes, try to be patient and try to understand the situation from their point of view.

If it still bothers you, try to talk to them about it. Not during heated discussions but instead when everyone is calm. Expressing your thoughts and emotions is also important, trying to convey your thoughts to them, only then will they get to know where they are going wrong and how to fix it.

You should also know what they are going through at the moment that is causing them to act as such. It is also important not to be too dependent on your parents, always going after them for your work and helping you. In the future, it will be hard for you to live independently.

If you stay independent and do well, you can prove to them that you are capable and have the ability to do things by yourself without them always having to nag you to do things. If you are hurt by your parent's words, it is okay to take a step back and let yourself heal and calm down because when you are hurt or in a stage of agony, there are many things you can do in anger that you could possibly regret later.

Going and talking to your parents about it, telling them that something that they had said hurt you, is helpful when you are ready to express your emotions. Based on the level of words they have used, you should try forgiving them while listening to their perspectives of the situation and the reason they said certain things. When your parents don't see the potential in you, it can be frustrating.

First off, you should know your potential, and believing in it is important ----> self-belief. Whenever you make new achievements or milestones, be sure to tell your parents about it. Showing you are doing well and that you can do better, showing your potential and determination. They will be impressed, guaranteed. In the future, when picking career paths or just general choices, your parents may not always support your decisions, you should know to try to give them time sometime, they might come around.

Stay strong and keep doing what you love. Showing you are responsible can show them that you are capable of many things, thus showing your potential in many ways. It can be challenging when parents don't see your potential but know you should always stay by your side, meaning always having trust in yourself.

Making mistakes is normal, but the important thing is that you should admit to it and try to fix it. Lying does not help in any situation whatsoever, especially to your parents, because they will obviously know when you lie to them. When I was younger, I used to sometimes lie about the smallest things, it's quite absurd, and guess what? That lying never paid off, I would still always get in trouble. Sometimes, it wasn't even because of what I did, instead, I would lie about such a petite matter.

If you have made a serious error, first of all, you should reflect upon it and try to realise what went wrong and why you did it. When our parents tell us they are disappointed in us, it hurts quite a bit more than an insult from them. Because they put all their trust in us, they believe we will do well, and when we do not, they are disappointed.

In the night, getting scolded because you just started to do an assignment that is due in 2 hours. They will obviously get mad because you are being irresponsible and you didn't do your work. We should try to understand what they are trying to convey and not always try to find faults in what they say.

Am I too less, is the thought that often comes into people's l heads after they do something that caused their parents to be extremely angry that it must have caused some kind of impact on the child. It makes them question a lot of things. When a child is going through something hectic that brings them a lot of stress, they sometimes question why they are here. Having these thoughts is not good, it is a serious topic that, if you have one, you should talk to someone about it. Don't keep thoughts like this bottled up, you should let your feelings out to someone once in a while. They can help you.

Trying to focus on the positive aspects of life is also better, nobody's life is perfect, and you should know that. Staying inside your room all day watching your phone all day is a typical stereotype of teens, at one point, parents notice you are on your phone a bit more often than before, and you stay inside your room most of the time and come out sometimes.

They sometimes start overthinking that you aren't involved in anything wrong in school or if you are okay mentally. Sometimes, it's good to let them know about what's going on in your life, it makes them feel more secure and happy that you guys are spending time together.

Chapter : 8

Relating to others

'The better we understand people,
the better we can relate to them.'

Relating to people brings comfort to people. Meaning it feels good to know that in any situation you are in now, you are not alone at all. It makes you feel like you can go up to that person and share what you feel about that situation, and you both can help each other out.

Relating, it can be viewed in many aspects, it can be comforting, bringing empathy towards others and building trust. Relating is a key factor in communication. Relating does not always mean finding someone who is going through the same situation as you, it could be sharing similar interests and experiences. How does relating help one?

When it's family, you can find so many people and situations to relate with. With family, you can have fun, enjoy and be yourself, so you can be open towards them, you can share your thoughts and remarks based on events, so they are also open with you, and they can also express their thoughts, eventually, you both will find so many similarities and common interests between each other. This can help you become good friends, learn from each other and just have someone to rely on.

It is necessary for you to relate to someone in life, it helps enlighten your thinking and brings new ideas and new perspectives to different situations. Through relating, we build relationships, in a way, when they relate to us, they pay more attention to you, and they are interested in starting a bond with you because of the relationship between both of you.

What exactly does relating to someone mean? It basically means being able to understand someone and building relationships. Relating with others also means being able to view a certain situation from their perspective. Trying to put yourself in someone else's shoes and being empathic towards them helps you relate well to someone.

Paying attention to someone and not being fake towards them is also important, it shows that you are genuinely interested in them and not just listening to them for the sake of listening to them. The person who you are speaking with feels good, it makes them feel as though they have someone to talk to them. One thing to pay attention to is when conversing with them, try not to get too carried away talking about yourself, focus on them more.

When meeting someone new, don't always keep the mindset that you have to always agree with them, and they always have to agree with you. Everyone is different, and everyone thinks in unique ways. Avoid trying to change that mindset of someone just so they agree with what you say.

Remember, everything good takes time, thus it's the same for a good relationship. Building a relationship takes time, it's normal if someone asks for time instead of heading headfirst into trying to maintain a good relationship with someone. Trust is important for a relationship to work, and that doesn't happen overnight. Showing that you are trustworthy is necessary, then only will they know that you are reliable and they can share things with you. You should know not to force someone to speak about something they aren't ready to.

When you notice someone lonely, go up to them and try to strike up a conversation, small talk as they say. They are mostly not going to be open as soon as you meet, so it's better if you try to be interactive with them, you can share things with them until they are comfortable with you.

It feels good to be cared about and loved by someone. Treat someone the way you want to be treated, with love and respect.

Finding courageous and strong-willed people, you can take inspiration from them. Talking to them about their qualities and mindset can teach you new things.

In a classroom, when a teacher is teaching, and the students are sitting with blank expressions on their faces, it's obvious they aren't able to understand what the teacher is trying to say. All the information is going through one ear and coming out the other. The students are bored. Why? Because the teacher isn't able to make the class interesting, and why is that? It's because the teacher is not able to relate with the students. It shows the teacher is not able to engage properly with the students. She isn't able to understand what to do so that the students have fun or are able to understand the lesson properly. If the teacher tries to have fun with the children, even attempts to relate to the children, pay attention to their interests.

Relating to someone is sharing passion or interest towards a topic with that person. Shared interests are good foundations for building great relationships.

Relating doesn't always mean finding similarities. Relating

is also just trying to make good and friendly relationships. When starting, find anything that you both like. So, you have something to talk about and share your thoughts about the same topic. You should know to respect their opinions, too. It is good to take part in activities that can involve both your interests.

If you show enthusiasm towards the topic the both of you are discussing about, it is good as then they will feel excited as well about the topic, and you can have better conversations. This will engage the other more in your conversations and the topic you are discussing about.

If you notice someone has a certain passion for a topic, make sure to encourage them and encourage them to reach for their goal. Everyone brings different views into the light, so you should be open to new feedback and views as you can learn from their experience.

Make sure to ask them questions if you are ever confused about any topic you are discussing, and actively listen to them so they know you are paying attention to them.

Relating on social media, there are ways to view this, two aspects to be specific. The good side is that it's all those social media creators you can relate to on a whole other level. There are many YouTubers that people can relate to and have fun watching. Other than that, there are mainly many creators online who give health tips, tips for exercising and basically anything you look for, arts and crafts, embroidery or playing musical instruments.

Anything you want, there are people for it. People online can teach maths, science, social, any subject basically, even coding courses. These are positive aspects of social media that can benefit people, help them in life, develop skills, learn new things and broaden their perspectives.

The negative aspects essentially are unrealistic standards. By unrealistic standards, I mean a certain standard is set about how your body should look, leading to body dissatisfaction and low self-esteem. But I am not saying this is the case for everyone, some people are genuine, while others are not.

On Instagram, people have the most fit body, they post pics of their food, which is salads and just fruits with healthy smoothies. When people see this and then look at themselves, they feel like they aren't pretty enough, or they aren't thin enough, etc. It created unrealistic beauty standards, especially for women. It makes them feel dissatisfied with themselves and brings down their confidence.

Studies show that the viewers who are most affected by social media body images are teen girls, as they spend more time on social media, it leads to body dissatisfaction, which is harmful. This is because people can go to an extent just to look like people on social media. For example, they starve themselves just to look thinner. People develop eating disorders.

If you look up **BMC Women's Health,**[1] they conducted in-depth interviews of teen girls [14-17 years old], it showed that their body image was a major concern. It had shown that the girls would change their appearances just to seek validation on social media. Girls count their appearance as their value. If they don't look good enough as other girls online or don't fit into beauty standards, there are no limits to what they would do just to look like others online.

Posts online create insecurity among teens. It causes anxiety, lowers body esteem and can cause mental health issues. Some even go into a state of depression just because they don't think they look good enough.

Negative impacts take place, going all the way to young teens even committing suicide. Sometimes, stereotypes of girls' bodies online can impact a girl too.

---

1 https://bmcwomenshealth.biomedcentral.com/articles/10.1186/s12905-022-01845-4

It is shown that girls watching movies with strong female leads impact them positively because, by the time girls become teens, they feel less brave and less confident.

In conclusion, relating to others is a part of life, but we need to be mindful that it can have negative impacts that take a toll on us. It brings us happiness and comfort, but we should be aware of who the people are and what we are relating to.

Chapter : 9

I am enough

Self-acceptance is key.

'I am enough', that doesn't mean you are perfect the way you are or you don't need to grow more in life. It means whatever happens in life, you can always change & improve, you should always look for your own growth, but that doesn't mean you should doubt yourself. " I am enough " doesn't mean being overconfident, but it gives you confidence that you can do things you want to do. Self-acceptance gives you confidence, it helps you to recognise your abilities and your potential. Self-acceptance can help make you more immune to criticism.

Everyone is unique, it is necessary for everyone to embrace themselves for who they are. Everyone is imperfectly perfect; nobody is just perfect in every way. Doubting yourself is normal, questioning yourself is natural. Like when you study really hard for a test, hoping for high results, but then getting low marks makes you doubt yourself. You think that you aren't good enough and start thinking, "This isn't for me.", and then just give up. You begin to develop a wrong mindset of simply giving up without having any motivation to try again and work harder.

A real-life example of mine, since my younger grades, I have always thought I was bad at mathematics. No, because I was seriously, really bad at it. My dad did try to help a lot, he would make me practice with him just so I could get better, but in my mind, I had made it final that I just wasn't ever going to be good at math.

Until 2 years back, I started tutoring online. My teacher was really good, but I still thought there was no point and I couldn't do it. Until I realised, I was finding it easy for the first time, and I understood it. She believed in me, and so did my dad, they believed that I would be able to do well. I put in my efforts, too, trying to learn and practice whatever she was teaching, and because of that, my thinking has started to change. I was finally able to do math without struggling that much and built more confidence.

If I hadn't put in any effort, and just stuck to that thinking that I was never going to be able to do math properly, would I have made it here? Obviously not. Sometimes, it's necessary to believe in yourself, even when times seem tough, and nothing seems to be working out for you. Always try to do your best and give it your all.

Don't try to change the things that make you unique. Being unique means being different, being different from others, meaning you are special. Don't try to hide it, and don't hate it.

My hair is something that makes me stand out, especially when I was younger. My hair is short and very curly, so when I was younger, it wasn't a very common hairstyle to see kids have. I thought the standard hairstyle for girls was just straight hair, and I thought my hair was very much not fitting that standard. So, I thought it was weird, and I let others tell me how it was different from any other ‘normal ’ hairstyle. In turn, I never really liked my hair. I was once even bullied because of it.

But as a kid, I didn't pay too much attention to my hair when it was short, when the pandemic hit and my hair grew longer, I was set with that hairstyle for 2 years. But then, last year, before my birthday, I got it cut into the same short haircut like I used to have as a kid because my mom preferred my old hair more, and she thought it looked better. Obviously, at first, I was very reluctant, saying there was no way I was going to get that haircut again.

But in the end, I decided to go. Well, I was very unhappy

after I got my haircut because I was so not used to looking at myself with short hair. Oh, I bawled my eyes out on the trip back home. After a few weeks, when it started to grow out a bit, I sort of liked it. And as time went on, I actually really liked it.

I was not willing to get the haircut because I didn't want to go through that whole short hair phase again because I thought I looked bad. But for once, I liked it. So, thanks to my mom for that.

A funny incident that took place a few months ago after I cut my hair again, there was a small carnival outside near my house, so I went out with my mom. Turns out one of her friends was there, and well, her friend mistook me for a boy and said, "Oh, is this your son?".

I used to be very conscious of my hair, and I always thought of what others would think of it. But now, maturing and growing up, I realise that's what makes me unique. I feel confident, I embrace it, I am unique, and I've accepted it. Now people are fascinated, all my aunties come and compliment my hair when I go to India, I feel good now.

Now, curly hair is a running trend as well, a media trend change. Now, there are more curly-haired models, too, showing what makes them unique. You are good enough the way you are, don't try to change yourself. Accept yourself for who you are.

One of my cousins was tall, like really tall. She used to be really conscious and insecure about her height. She would always think of herself as the odd one out, like the one taller than average. And others didn't make it easy for her, they unintentionally pointed out her height many times during conversations, and she became even more conscious.

I would see her every few months, and she would get taller until she reached 17-18 years old. She had a profound interest in basketball, so when she joined her college, she joined the basketball team and became the captain. Soon, in her second or third year, she joined the fashion team. She took part in many fashion shows at her college, and everyone absolutely loved her. She had the perfect height for a model. And wow, her catwalk was awesome.

See, nobody is perfect, and we have to accept the fact that we all have flaws, and it's normal. What's important is that we should love ourselves either way. We all have a purpose in life, don't doubt yourself when times get tough. Never question your worth. Always know to get back up, always try harder and never give up, always believe in yourself. You don't need to be perfect to be accepted by society. You should know your own worth. Value your worth as an individual without waiting for others' validation, and don't compare yourself to others.

We should love and appreciate the person we are today, for we have worked hard to reach wherever we are today. You should hold on to the belief that you are enough. You deserve all the happiness and good things that happen in life, these will guide you to realise your self-worth. Self-acceptance is not ignoring your self-worth, instead, it's acknowledging our imperfections.

www.ingramcontent.com/pod-product-compliance
Lightning Source LLC
LaVergne TN
LVHW091119150826
845673LV00002B/891

* 9 7 8 9 3 6 0 0 6 5 4 0 9 *